How to Discipline Your Mind

Excel at Focused Decision-Making in a Distracted World

By Zoe McKey

zoemckey@gmail.com

www.zoemckey.com

to in this work as a citation and/or potential source of further information does not mean that the author endorses the information the individual, organization, or website may provide or recommendations they/it may make. Further, readers should be aware that Internet websites listed in this work might have changed or disappeared between when this work was written and when it was read.

Please contact the author for general information on the products and services or to obtain technical support.

Thank you for choosing my book!

I would like to show my appreciation for the trust you gave me by giving a **GIFT** to you!

>> CLICK HERE TO GET MY SELF-DISCOVERY STARTER KIT <<

The kit shares *10 key practices to help you to:*

- *discover your true self,*
- *find your life areas that need improvement,*
- *find self-forgiveness,*
- *become better at socializing,*
- *lead a life of gratitude and purpose.*

The kit contains extra actionable worksheets with practice exercises for deeper learning.

Visit www.zoemckey.com and get your copy NOW!

Table of Contents

Introduction   11

Chapter 1: Everything In Life Is A Tradeoff   25

Chapter 2: On Responsibility   41

Chapter 3: Learn To Question What You Think
You Know   49

Chapter 4: Body Language   57

Chapter 5: How To Cope With Stress Effectively?
                                                            67

Chapter 6: Be At Peace With Your Virtual Life 87

Chapter 7: Know Thyself   101

Chapter 8: Pay Attention To What Thoughts You
Feed   113

Chapter 9: Failing And Learning   121

Chapter 10: Practice, Practice, Practice   131

Closing Thoughts   145

One Last Thing…   151

Other Books By Zoe   155

Reference   165

Endnotes   171

Introduction

"Grant me the serenity to accept the things I cannot change, courage to change the things I can, and wisdom to know the difference."
– Serenity Prayer, Reinhold Niebuhr

Once upon a time, my life took a significant turning point. Leaving behind Romania, my home country, I set my course to pursue better opportunities in Hungary, armed with nothing but a hard-earned scholarship. My parents weren't made of money. Hence a rented apartment was a luxury we couldn't afford. Consequently, I found myself nestled in the high school's free dormitory.

Just as you'd expect, the free dorm provided the basics – a roof overhead, showers, a wardrobe, and a bed. Nothing more. Before you start brainstorming what else I would need, I'll give you a hint: food was not included. "At least I can bathe before I die of hunger," I thought with a hint of teenage melodrama.

It was not the school's problem that I couldn't afford the cheap canteen meals in the dorm's kitchen, which were tailored to feed poor kids. But I was a notch below the previously mentioned socio-economic status, the extreme end of the poverty bell curve, within my school's demographic. Yet, I held on to my dignity like a lifeline, my head held high, refusing to ask for help. I saw myself as a warrior – a survivor – I can deal with life's stuff.

I "dealt" with the problem by sulking in the kitchen at lunchtime, watching the others eat, hoping that someone would just walk away indefinitely from their lunch. That never happened. The best I could hope for was some leftovers. Even then, my foolish pride kept me fasting instead of feasting, as I was worried someone else would see me. I was your typical self-conscious teenager. I would reason on Friday, "No, I'm not hungry. I've eaten already… this week." So I just sat, sulked, and prayed the canteen lady didn't clean up the leftovers before I could.

I spent three days hoping that if I stayed around the dining hall long enough, I would get some food without the added shame of exposure. But I didn't. The only thing I noticed besides my growling stomach was the canteen lady's constant lament about the dishes.

Aha – a lightbulb moment!

The next day, after lunchtime was over, I started collecting the dishes in the dining hall, carrying them back to the serving deck where the canteen lady would wash them. She was taken aback by my willingness to help. As she was expressing her gratitude, my stomach, like a well-trained dog, started growling loudly at just the right moment, sending a clear message to the mother of three. Understanding the universal language of hunger, she immediately offered me more leftovers than I knew what to do with. From that moment on, I had a job and a payment, earning my meal through kitchen labor.

I often harken back to the nugget of wisdom shared at the start of this chapter. It wasn't in my power to change the schooling system in Hungary, to insist on including free meals alongside free tuition and housing. The solution to my problem was right in front of me, and luckily, I saw and took the opportunity to change what I could. The impact was great and immediate.

The things you can't change are the things you can't control.

Consequently, the things we can change are those that fall under our control. We want to feel in control; it's human. When they're not, desperation often sets in. In this state, we lose sight of potential solutions right in front of us.

With a nod to Niebuhr's words, I found my mantra: Grant me the serenity to accept the things I *cannot control,* the courage to change the things I *can control*, and the wisdom to know the difference.

Much of our control-related frustrations are rooted in our inability to clearly discern our circle of influence.[i] We are the protagonists of our lives, but that doesn't guarantee our wishes will invariably be met. And that's okay. What we can choose are our beliefs and principles. A deep understanding of these principles is key to better decision-making.

In his best-selling book *The 7 Habits of Highly Effective People,* Stephen Covey discusses useful principles one can live by. One of these principles is proactivity.

We are unique creatures, gifted with the ability to introspect, mold our self-image, and determine our reactions to our circumstances. We hold the reins of our effectiveness. To harness this power, Covey suggests being proactive, not reactive. What's the difference?

Reactive folks are passengers of life, convinced that the world is happening to them. Phrases such as "That's just how I am," "There's nothing I can do about it," or "I can't" are their anthems. Their problems are "out there," vast and daunting, leaving them feeling helpless. The real obstacle, though, is this very mindset, as reactivity tends to weave its self-fulfilling prophecy. As reactive individuals perceive themselves as victims, they tend not to act to resolve their issues. And so, the issues persist, validating their original presumption: they were indeed powerless.

On the flip side, proactive people are aware of their responsibility—or as Covey phrases it, "response-ability." It's the capacity to choose our responses to stimuli. As psychiatrist and Holocaust survivor Victor Frankl suggests, there is a fleeting moment between the stimulus and response that holds the power to determine our reaction.

"I decide and control my reactions."
"Let me see the alternatives."
"I choose."

Covey introduces the concepts of the Circle of Concerns (a larger circle) and the Circle of Influence (a smaller circle within the big one). He states that we should focus on our Circle of Influence – the aspects we can effectively change. In other words, we should invest time and energy responsibility to apologize and possibly pay for the dry cleaning.

Life often throws curveballs where you bear no fault for the misfortune. If, for example, you learn that your baby may be born with a severe illness, it's certainly not your fault. But the responsibility to make a decision—and to bear the consequences of that decision for the rest of your life—falls squarely on your shoulders.

The more responsibility you take, the more control you exert over your life, thereby expanding your Circle of Influence. Why? As soon as you accept responsibility for something, you jump from the past to the present. Issues get solved in the present.

What are the steps to maximize your control in a situation?

1. Know the outcome you want.

2. Anticipate unexpected events that could delay or circumvent your plans.

3. Stay flexible in your path to your goal.

4. Be open to revising the goal.

5. Own your responsibility.

You can apply these steps to minor issues as well as larger problems. Practicing to maximize control and habitually take responsibility demands conscious effort. Make mental (or written) notes of your reactions to stress-inducing scenarios. Do your reactions align with your values? Can you maintain your composure? Are you operating from your Circle of Influence?

Consider which areas of life challenge your sense of control and responsibility the most. What situations incite defensiveness, anger, or discouragement in you? What elements of your Circle of Concern are you fueling? Familiarize yourself with these aspects of your current personality; awareness is the first step toward growth.

Write your self-assessment down the following way:

1. These are the events I react to that fall within my Circle of Concerns:

   -

   -

   -

   -

2. When I feel I'm out of control, I usually react the following way:

   -

   -

   -

   -

3. These are the immediate changes I want to make to be more aligned with my values and to operate from my Circle of Influence:

   -

   -

   -

   -

Key takeaways to discipline your mind:

- The things you can change are those that fall under your Circle of Influence. Change them to best fit your life.

- Taking responsibility for your actions doesn't mean accepting culpability.

- Get to know your reactions and change the ones that lie in your Circle of Concerns.

Chapter 1: Everything in Life is a Tradeoff

The abundance of choices we have today can be a double-edged sword. On the one hand, we've never had more options in terms of careers, lifestyles, travel destinations, and even restaurants. On the other hand, the very abundance of options can lead to a sense of paralysis, dissatisfaction, or constant second-guessing. It has never been easier to travel to Fiji. Or Tahiti. Or the Great Coral Reef. You have seven days and $5,000. Which one will you choose? Unless it was your long-cherished dream to travel to either of these destinations, you'll sit down in disappointment and shake your head, feeling stronger about the options you're discarding than the one you're settling on. Have you ever felt this way?

countless others. While assessing your needs and prioritizing them is smart, getting lost in constant opportunity cost analysis is a shortcut to stress and burnout. So how do we navigate this labyrinth of choices without losing our minds?

Mark Manson, the bestselling author of *The Subtle Art of Not Giving a F*ck*, wrote a blog post based on a story shared by CTV News, Canada. [iv] Mohammed El-Erian, the CEO of the two trillion-dollar worth bond fund PIMCO, was pulling in a decent $100 million per year salary and an upward-running career. Some might say he had it all.

El-Erian stunned the world when he decided to resign from his position. Why would he do that, you might ask? What can be better than a $100 million salary? Maybe a $200 million? Nope. Finding a better-paying job was not his reason for quitting. He wanted to spend more quality time with his ten-year-old daughter.

Of course, news like this doesn't go unnoticed in our society. It sparked a wildfire of interest, defying our society's obsession with wealth building. The tipping point for El-Erian was an argument with his daughter over brushing her teeth. His demand was met with defiance, to which his response was, "I'm your father, and you will do what I say." Hearing her father's reasoning, the little girl wrote a list of twenty-two moments of her life in the current year when her father was absent because of work. Understanding the loss of the priceless, precious moments flipped a switch in El-Erian, and he resigned from his lucrative job and embraced his role as a father.

Therein lies the essence of opportunity cost; you can have anything but can't have everything. Especially not all at once. But patience and decisiveness can help. Take the donkey, for example. It would still be alive if it settled on eating for ten minutes and then drinking. Derek

Sivers, thinker and the author of *Anything You Want*, says, "If you're thirty now and have six different directions you want to pursue, then you can do each one for ten years and have done all of them by the time you're ninety. It seems ridiculous to plan to age ninety when you're thirty, right? But it's probably coming, so you might as well take advantage of it. You can fully focus on one direction at a time without feeling conflicted or distracted because you know you'll get to the others."

Patience is a virtue and a pathway to fulfillment. Satisfy your hunger and then your thirst. Be patient and mindful about how time works – you can do a lot over time. Go to Fiji, learn Mandarin, and eat pizza this time. And you can have a great time in Tahiti, hone your communication skills, and eat sushi the next time. Except, you'll likely still be learning Mandarin because it's one tough language!

Every choice you make is also a sacrifice. For El-Erian, he chose his daughter over his job. The bolder the choice, the bigger "opportunity cost" you have to pay. High-profile people are admired in our society for their money and success. What people don't see is the opportunity cost behind their achievements. Bill Gates was famous for sleeping in his office, and Angelina Jolie can't make a step without being photographed or harassed by the media. But remember, these were their choices, and they willingly took on the associated opportunity cost.

So next time you're in the YOLO-FOMO tug-of-war, remember that life isn't about having all at once. It's about prioritizing what matters most, being patient, and embracing your choices wholeheartedly. It's your life, your journey – navigate it with courage and authenticity.

Time is our most precious asset.

It's non-renewable, non-negotiable, and we can't get it back once spent. Spending time, therefore, naturally attracts the expectation of a reward. When you spend your time working, you expect money. When you wash the dishes in the canteen, you expect dinner. It's an unspoken rule, a balance of give and take. Welcome to the Law of Reciprocity.

Rarely do people do something for nothing. Why? Because they are investing their most valuable non-renewable resource, time. When we invest our time in something, we expect to get something out of it. Similarly, when others spend their time on us, we feel an almost instinctive pull to reciprocate.

Do you ever find yourself in compliment ping-pong? Someone compliments you, "Your hair looks so gorgeous." Almost reflexively, you start scanning them to repay the compliment, "Oh, and I absolutely love your dress." This, of course, is a small-scale exchange, but it well reflects the Law of Reciprocity at work. Social psychologists define this law as the intrinsic urge to give back when someone does something for you. Sometimes you even feel compelled to amplify your response - you get one muffin and give two muffins in return. Some people resist this urge, but it often results in feelings of guilt or shame.

Reciprocity can also veer into negative territory. In layman's terms, we call this revenge. It's a natural psychological urge – for the better or worse. However, in our civilized society, we aim to suppress this instinct. While the Code of Hammurabi, written in 1754 BC by the sixth Babylonian king Hammurabi, was actively proposing the "eye for eye and teeth for teeth"[v] principle, the Judeo-Christian, Buddhist, and other religious traditions came forth with a different approach to revenge. They were spreading the wisdom of tolerance, "turning the other cheek," or as the Filipino saying goes, "if someone throws a stone at you, throw back also, but with bread instead of stone." There has been a shift in negative reciprocity over the centuries. However, in some cultures, the concept of "vendetta" is still very much alive. Generally speaking, positive reciprocity is encouraged to cultivate a disciplined mind, while negative reciprocity is discouraged.

The Law of Reciprocity can be used for manipulation. Some people might shower you with compliments and offer unsolicited favors, intending to leverage your instinctive urge to reciprocate. Be aware of this and listen to your gut when you feel like someone approached you in dishonesty:

- What are the potential benefits and drawbacks for me? And for them?
- How does the balance of give and take feel? Am I comfortable with it?
- Could there be hidden motives behind this person's actions?

If you are satisfied with the give-and-take exchange, reciprocal interaction can be mutually beneficial. If you feel that you'd end up with the shorter end of the stick, make an informed decision with this awareness.

Keep in mind that your time is your most valuable opportunity cost asset. Guard it wisely.

How costly is opportunity anyway? How can we make the best value-based decision about our time?

Mark Manson contemplates, "What if the solution is simply accepting our bounded potential, our unfortunate tendency as humans to inhabit only one place in space and time? What if we recognize our life's inevitable limitations and then prioritize what we care about based on those limitations?"[vi]

People who often complain about their jobs, lack of time, stagnation, and lack of direction usually don't know what the real priorities in their life are.

Do you know yours? What is your most significant life goal? What are you willing to sacrifice to achieve it? Where do you draw the line? There is no correct answer to these questions. Find what's the most important goal for you and focus your time and energy accordingly.

Perhaps you equally value family and career. There is nothing wrong with that. As we established already, you can achieve different goals at different times. While you can't have everything at once, you can always have something. Just remember El-Erian.

To trigger the Law of Reciprocity, we need to give first to start to get.

Let me share a personal story. One day I found a wallet filled with cash. An insidious inner voice whispered, "Take the money! You won't have to wash dishes for weeks!" However, another, more virtuous voice countered, "Take a look at this old wallet. Someone worked hard for that money. How could you take that away? You have the possibility to eat. If you take the money, this person might not have that chance." Resenting the voice of virtue, I decided to take a look for an ID in the wallet, hoping to see a twenty-year-old yuppie who just lost his lunch money. Instead, I recognized a middle-aged man who regularly conducted Aikido classes at my school.

I went to the gym to return his wallet. He was very surprised by that. We started talking, and it turned out he was a third-dan Aikido master. While telling me stories about the Aikido philosophy, he noticed a glow of interest in my eyes. He asked me to join his class.

- You can have everything you want, just not at the same time.
- Give before you expect to get something.
- Give more than you get. This way, you'll get more than you expect.
- Have clarity about what you want to make more informed choices and not be so affected by the burden of opportunity costs.

Chapter 2: On Responsibility

Most Westerners are the children of a generation born into extraordinary liberty – the freedom of speech, freedom of self-expression, and yes, even free Wi-Fi. We're the beneficiaries of a lot of advantages that have been earned through the sacrifice and blood of our ancestors. Today in we can access everything so easily, with so little sacrifice that we don't even consider how privileged we are – rather, we tend to take things for granted. We feel entitled to these things even though we did nothing to earn them. Easy gains attract existential issues that can be at odds with having a disciplined mind.

The More Syndrome.

People take things for granted and constantly crave more. This tendency can become harmful if not tempered with awareness. It can make us brittle in spirit and lazy at resilience. If today's best becomes the baseline for tomorrow, we risk turning our lives into a battleground of unmet desires and unrealistic expectations and hopes.

The entitlement epidemic.

You are entitled to your property, beliefs, and other things you earned. The problem arises when entitlement extends beyond its rightful domain. When people believe they have a right to something by default, without earning it – legally or morally – they are treading dangerous waters. Even in instances where the claim may be legitimate (for example, everyone has the right to enjoy a public park), a sense of entitlement without appreciation leads to taking things for granted. In relationships, the issue of entitlement can raise even more troubles, like one party feeling entitled to loving affection even if they behave poorly. And then, entitled people – those who feel the world owes them something - are not great at taking responsibility.

The world is not responsible for you. You're responsible for yourself in the world.

At age fifteen, I grappled with navigating my new life in Hungary without any knowledge of money management or local regulations. I was a teenager who nobody took seriously; people often told me to "bring your parents." But I had no parents around.

One day, my school required a document confirming my permanent residence in the country. Despite my confusion over what this meant, I sought advice from the only familiar adult around me, the canteen lady. She suggested visiting the immigration office, which presented a bureaucratic catch-22. The immigration office demanded confirmation of my legal studies from the school, and the school needed the residency document from the immigration office. To make matters worse, my father couldn't help or travel to Hungary due to financial constraints.

The situation was frustrating and unfair. I felt abandoned and helpless, caught in a bureaucratic loophole. *"Last year, I played with Barbie dolls, and now this?"* (I was a late bloomer in a different era.) My predicament forced me to take control of my situation and act responsibly. After all, my problems were no one else's, and nobody could do it in my place. Realizing my knowledge gap, I spent hours every day researching. This wasn't easy, and I often questioned why I had to deal with such nonsense. But my desperation forced me to accept the harsh realities of my life – I'm alone - and find solutions.

One day, I found an article discussing "temporary residence" for foreign students. Armed with this newfound knowledge, I returned to the immigration office, demanded the document I needed, and submitted it to my school. My school filled out the papers, which I took back to the immigration office, and finally, I got my temporary residency card. This early lesson taught me the importance of personal responsibility and self-advocacy in the face of adversity.

In retrospect, the solution was incredibly simple, and something immigration officials should have known. Maybe they knew it, or it was something that would have taken them five minutes to look up.

However, people don't have five minutes for your problems when they don't have five minutes for their own.

When you seek help, it's good to keep in mind that people often don't have the bandwidth to tackle their issues, let alone yours. While some might help, to hinge your life's stability on the whims of others is like building a castle in the sand. You couldn't control the waves, constantly worrying about tide changes, tied to the mercy of the weather.

The old adage, "Freedom isn't free," while primarily associated with justifying wartime efforts, is equally applicable to daily life. The freedom to make choices and enjoy personal security often requires sacrifice, such as dedicating time to find your own solutions and embracing full responsibility for your actions.

How can you handle a challenge responsibly without relying on external forces to save you? Here are some self-reflective questions to guide you in independently addressing your problems:

1. What is the challenge I'm facing?

2. Why is it a challenge?

3. What do I already know about it, and what do I need to learn?

4. What is the worst possible outcome?

5. What can I do to avoid the worst-case scenario?

6. What outcome am I seeking?

7. What can I do now to get to my desired outcome?

I'm not saying never ask for help or that people will never help you. They often will. But, as the Law of Reciprocity states, they will expect something in return. For genuine peace of mind, feeling in command of your life is essential. This control is achieved by understanding your problems and having faith in your ability to solve them, even if you delegate some of the tasks.

Key takeaways to discipline your mind:

- Take responsibility for your problems because nobody else will.

- People don't have five minutes for your problems when they don't have five minutes for themselves.

- You don't have to solve all your problems by yourself. You can rely on others. However, knowing that you could solve your issues if you wanted to gives you peace of mind.

Chapter 3: Learn to Question What You Think You Know

As a child, I believed my grandparents when they told me eating carrots would help me whistle better and that would attract pigeons. (As a kid, I really loved pigeons.) I also believed spinach made me stronger, though I was wary of ending up with disproportionately large forearms like Popeye.

When I moved away from home, I told everybody that I was okay. I tried to believe that too. In truth, I was lonely and scared. I believed that if I wore more fashionable clothes and acted cooler, I'd win people's admiration and interest.

When I had my first boyfriend, I believed we'd always be together; eternal love in a quaint cottage in the woods, a slew of cats, and enduring happiness stemming merely from our togetherness. When we broke up, I believed I'd never love anybody as much as I loved him – and nobody would love me as he did. Then I had another boyfriend who loved me much more. And then another.

My beliefs were misguided all the way from carrots to love.

I'm sure that if I look back five years from now at my current beliefs, I will realize some were off the mark. I hope I will. It's a sign of growth, an indication that I'll be wiser in the future.

I don't think there is a universal definition of right or wrong. These labels are often personal, based on individual values and experiences. Not considering the extremely damaging, negative values that some people consider right, we can largely agree that the notions of "right" or "wrong" are subjective.

People's perspectives and values can diverge, leading to different answers to the same questions. None of those answers is inherently better or worse than another, as long as it doesn't harm someone else's freedom to share their own view. Our answers might be different today than what we said a decade ago. It's a testament to our ever-evolving journey of growth and understanding.

Humans have a superpower, the ability to think and think about our thoughts and emotions. Ideally, this exceptional power should equip us to maintain emotional balance, handle every problem individually (not mixing past with present), and devise well-thought-out solutions. But without deliberate mindfulness, our brains often resort to default modes, trawling through our emotional archives and fishing out a previously applied solution to a similar circumstance. This one-size-fits-all problem-solving often gets us in trouble because each situation is different and would require a response conceived in the present.

For example, imagine that your ex-partner cheated on you, and you exposed their infidelity through secret phone chats. Post such trauma, it's natural for you to be hypersensitive to any future partner being engrossed in their phone. If left unchecked, your brain on autopilot mode will release an emergency troop of emotions to deal with the threatening situation. Your new partner might feel offended by your lack of trust, leading to conflict. Reacting to unique situations with the same solution will cause unnecessary turmoil.

The brain is an unpredictable organ, sometimes leading us to perceive things that aren't real and even rewrite our memory. A fascinating study showcased this – participants were shown holiday photos of Disneyland featuring Bugs Bunny mingling and shaking hands with children. After the slideshow was over, some subjects clearly remembered shaking Bugs Bunny's hand as well when they were in Disneyland. But Bugs Bunny is a Warner Brothers character. Thus, he was never in Disneyland.[vii]

Understanding the need to question our mental processes paves the way for better decision-making and, consequently, an enhanced quality of life.

How can you question your beliefs?

The goal here isn't necessarily changing your beliefs but understanding them better. When I was coaching, I encouraged my clients to critically examine their self-concepts and perceptions of the world. They aimed to identify and reflect on those that held them back. I usually asked these questions:

- When did you first adopt the belief _____? (Write down the belief.)

- Who taught you to believe that you _____? (Can or can't do something.)

- Did you ever question this belief? Did you research to confirm the validity of the belief? Did you ask others to confirm your belief?

- How would changing this belief impact your life? Would it affect someone else?

- Have you ever discussed this belief with someone holding a contrary viewpoint?

These questions can help you explore your beliefs and help you understand the beliefs of others in a constructive way.

It's essential to revisit your core beliefs periodically because you learn, improve, and experience novelty each day. Closer inspection might reveal that you are operating based on outdated beliefs. Questioning ingrained beliefs can be uncomfortable. Discarding those that no longer hold true can lead to personal betterment.

For example, I had a client who lost a significant amount of weight but continued to harbor beliefs tied to his previous self-image. Despite becoming fit and muscular, he remained reticent and timid for a long time, especially around women. He found it surprising when women would talk to him and even questioned their motives. It took time for him to reconcile his beliefs with his transformed physique.

Confronting and updating his obsolete beliefs helped my client to release some anxiety and open up to the question, "What's the worst that could happen if I went on a date with her?"

Despite the debates surrounding Mehrabian's percentages, the core idea remains valid: understanding body language gives us better awareness about the thoughts and feelings of others and ourselves. Body language provides a window into our genuine emotions that our brain might want to conceal.

For example, you can declare you're not afraid of heights, striving to convince yourself and those around you. Yet, your trembling legs, involuntary grip on a support, and frequent closing of your eyes betray your actual fear. Your body language is a telltale sign contradicting your words.

Inconsistent signals can erode credibility, whether the receiver consciously recognizes or merely senses the dissonance. When you meet somebody you haven't seen for a long time who welcomes you with a big smile but also has crossed arms, and their body turned towards the exit, you'll get the message that they're not as happy to see you as they claim.

Body language embodies our subconscious, while words often reflect our conscious mind. This doesn't mean our subconscious mind is "right." It's an emotional reflex system deeply rooted in past experiences and housing our instincts. Yet, it often mirrors emotions more authentically. So, if you're keen on understanding someone's thoughts, pay closer attention to their body language.

People do not always say what they truly think or feel. If you want to get to the bottom of someone's real feelings, you have to discover what's behind their words. While this book isn't a comprehensive guide to body language, it will highlight key aspects to help you uncover concealed emotions. For an in-depth study on body language, I recommend the works of Allan and Barbara Pease, such as *The Definitive Book of*

Body Language or *Signals* or Joe Navarro's book *What Every Body Is Saying.*

The key to deciphering emotions is to look for telltale signs. If somebody is crying, presumably, the person is sad, upset, or otherwise distressed. But tears can also be ones of joy if they appear along with laughter. Some tears are used to gain sympathy, thus creating an illusion of emotion. Always examine the context for a more accurate interpretation.

Expressions of anger, impatience, or anxiety often manifest through facial cues and body language. Facial expressions are the easiest to read, followed by body language, including personal space and posture. A person with crossed arms rhythmically tapping their foot is probably impatient. However, if they cross their arms, look downward, and shuffle their feet awkwardly, they're likely displaying anxiety or bashfulness.

How can you determine a fake smile? The first sign of a wholehearted smile lies in the eyes. In such a case, the lips will curve upward, and small wrinkles around the eyes will also appear. When we say "cheese" for the photographer, we seem to be smiling because the zygomatic muscles are pulled backward, leaving the eye untouched. It's the consummate fake smile.

In the animal kingdom, bared teeth don't always signify joy. A monkey's expression can convey fear, happiness, or aggression, but discerning among these requires looking into its eyes. The same is true with humans. If the eyes don't laugh, the grim can be deceptive.[x] Just think about the Joker in *The Dark Knight*. He was smiling… and slicing people's throats in the meantime.

Oh, those telltale eyes. There are a lot of verbal expressions referring to certain nonverbal eye communication. "He looks down on me," "icy stare," "bewitching glance," "look me in the eye," and so forth. The eyes are the mirror to the soul. With careful observation, a person's eyes can divulge their emotions even before they speak.

The eyes can be powerful tools of persuasion. Women often use the up-looking technique to convince men about something. (If you wonder what the up-looking technique looks like, google Princess Diana's signature girl-like glance photos.[xi] You know, where she shyly looks upward while keeping her chin down. True up-glance mastery…)

It is a common myth that liars struggle to maintain eye contact. However, many, aware of this stereotype, deliberately hold an unbreakable gaze. Signs that may expose deceit are twitching of the mouth, ear scratching, or inexplicable limb spasms.

Before body language assessment, always consider cultural differences. Some nonverbal cues are universal, but others can lead to significant misunderstanding if misread. If you plan to travel, do a quick search for the typical praising or insulting nonverbal signs in the country you will visit. For example, Facebook's famous signature "Like" sign (the thumbs-up image) in the Western world means "okay," "cool," "one," or a hitchhiking signal. In Greece, however, it means "go to hell," especially if it is moved up and down. In Japan, it means "five" or "man."[xii]

How can you enhance your body language reading skills?

Choose a good, old, black-and-white silent movie in a retro theater and try to predict what the characters will do next based solely on their mimics and gestures. Silent movies are excellent starters to observe body language because the lack of sounds makes the actors very expressive with their physiques.

When you can guess eight out of ten actions that follow in a silent movie, take your practice to the next level. Watch a regular movie with the sound off. This will be more challenging because spoken dialogue and sound effects often provide context for actions. When you can score eight of ten correct prognostications in muted "regular" movies, start reading the body language of the people around you.

Remember to consider the full picture. Don't jump to conclusions based on one or two signals, and most importantly, don't take your guessing as the ultimate truth. Reading body language is a skill that can help you understand others' feelings better, but it isn't an exact science.

Check your own body language occasionally and compare it to your conscious thoughts. Do they match? Don't forget. Body language expresses the unfiltered feelings of your subconscious. You can learn a lot about yourself if you choose to pay attention to them.

Key takeaway to discipline your mind:

- Learn to read the most common body language signs. You can get a much clearer picture of how others truly feel.

Chapter 5: How to Cope with Stress Effectively?

Stress is the body's response to perceived challenges or threats. When you face such situations, the nervous system reacts by releasing stress hormones like adrenaline and cortisol, which trigger a series of physiological changes designed to enhance your strength, sharpen your focus, and quicken your reactions – often referred to as a "fight or flight" response.[xiii]

What are the major causes of stress?

Stress can arise from a variety of sources, both external and internal. External stressors might include major life changes, workplace issues, financial problems, relationship struggles, or feeling generally overwhelmed. On the other hand, internal stressors can involve factors like a negative self-image, persistent worry, perfectionism, inflexibility, and extreme or black-and-white thinking.

There are different types of stress levels, which can be categorized as follows:

Sub-stress is a state of underlying stress you might not consciously acknowledge. Often, people experiencing sub-stress deny their feelings of stress, presenting a facade of indifference or detachment. For instance, they might downplay the impact of other people's opinions on them. However, continuously denying or suppressing stress can be detrimental and can prevent self-reflection and growth.

Optimal stress – Sometimes referred to as 'eustress,' this is a beneficial level of stress that can enhance performance. In this state, you are alert and prepared to face challenges. Your body is primed to bring out your full potential, and you might experience a rush of adrenaline. This kind of stress often precedes important events or tasks, like a job interview or a presentation. You're dancing on thin ice, though. This state can easily transform into the next category, the supra-stress phase.

Supra stress – This is the stress we hate. The one that paralyzes our brain numbs our limbs, and makes us feel miserable. When we face supra-stress, life becomes a struggle. In this state, you might feel overwhelmed, anxious, and unable to function effectively. Chronic exposure to supra-stress can take a toll on your physical and mental health and might make you fearful of stress.

Let's talk some more about the elephant in the room, supra-stress. It can be divided into three parts: manageable, partly manageable, and unmanageable.

There are those monolithic stressors that feel like Mount Everest in your path. They're *unmanageable*, unpredictable, unrelenting, and out of your control. This might be something as painful as a serious illness, the loss of a loved one, or a crisis that engulfs your nation. There's a raw, harsh reality here - you can't change them, you can't eliminate them. But what you can do is take a deep breath and accept them. It's tough, it hurts, but it's the only way to weather the storm. Allow yourself to feel the sorrow, shed the tears, grieve, and let the storm rage and wash over you. These issues lie outside your Circle of Influence, so the best you can do is to shift your mindset, embrace acceptance, and navigate the path forward.

Forgiveness and acceptance can ease the pain supra-stress causes. When you choose to forgive - be it yourself or others - for whatever sparked the stress, you'll feel as if a heavy burden has been lifted off your shoulders. This is your ticket to relief and a step toward healing.

Partly manageable stressors are the ones that tiptoe on the edges of your Circle of Influence. You can change your part in them since you have some control over them. For example, you might not be able to change the nature of your boss or your partner, but you do have the power to alter your perspective of the relationship. This might mean deliberately exercising more patience, embracing acceptance, biting your tongue before snapping or striving to understand better. As you start to transform your behavior, you might just inspire the other person to do the same. But regardless of their response, you'll find comfort in knowing that you're doing your best and being the person you aspire to be.

The smallest and, in many ways, the easiest to tackle are those pesky *manageable stressors*. This group is populated with thousands and thousands of little annoyances waiting to stress us out - being stuck in traffic, not finding your favorite snack in the store, or the WiFi going off. And yet, these daily irritants can build up like small bricks, constructing a wall of stress. But the good news? They can be knocked down! All it takes is a shift in attitude and a hearty dose of patience.

Take note; stress can be a real threat to both our physical and mental health. It can shake up your cognitive abilities, leading to memory problems, impaired judgment, persistent worrying, and a generally gloomy outlook. It can disrupt your daily habits, triggering eating and sleeping disorders or an increased reliance on substances like alcohol, drugs, or cigarettes. Emotional upheaval is another red flag - mood swings, a short fuse, feeling overwhelmed, an inability to relax, or sinking into depression. And let's not forget those physical symptoms - aches, nausea, frequent colds, and a racing heartbeat.

How can you handle stress better?

- First, identify your stressors.[xiv]

Kick-start your stress detective journey! Dig deep to identify your major stressors and place them in the right category. Are they hidden in the depths of sub-stress, swimming on the surface of optimal stress, or rising like mountains in the realm of supra-stress?

- Categorize supra-stress.

What kind of supra-stressors are you dealing with? Is it manageable, partly manageable, or unmanageable?

Deal with identifying and releasing unmanageable stressors first. You can't solve them or erase them, but you can learn to navigate around them. Is there someone you need to forgive? Or perhaps there's something you need to accept? Remember, you're not doing this for anyone else but for your peace of mind. When my grandparents passed away, I had to forgive myself for not being there as much as I wished I had. I realized I wasn't honoring their memory by drowning in guilt; instead, I chose to spend more quality time with my parents. That decision helped me let go of the stress and truly grieve. It's a bittersweet feeling but one that allows for healing.

Next, check your manageable stressors. The saying, choose your battles wisely, applies to these. The impact of manageable stressors is usually short-lived. Practice noticing what triggers these bursts of upheaval and try to find their root cause. If you're stressed in the line at the supermarket, is it because you don't have time (you can work on your time management) or because you find it indignant to stand in line, "this always happens to me, I always pick the wrong line" (it's not about you, lines just happen and people happen to get stuck in them – here working on not taking things so personally could help).

Lastly, collect your partly manageable stressors. This is usually the group that can bring the most distress into your life – especially if you don't take action to change what lies in your Circle of Influence. Doing what you can in such situations can diffuse the tension and help you feel at peace with yourself – "I did all I could, so whatever happens, happens." While there still might be residue anxiety for not knowing, owning your control zone will alleviate stress.

- Social connections.[xv]

Don't underestimate the power of social support in your battle against stress. Share your fears and challenges with your friends. Maintaining a stress journal can also work wonders. Pouring your heart out on paper can release tension, and revisiting your entries days later will help you realize how fleeting many of your stressors were. Hiring a therapist can be a game-changer too. Having someone there just to listen, guide, and ask the right questions can help untangle the messy web of emotions and stress.

- R.E.S.T.: Relax, Eat, Sleep, Train.

Mens sana in corpore sano, a Latin phrase, is translated as "a healthy mind in a healthy body." And it couldn't be more accurate! Regular Relaxation, mindful Eating, plenty of Sleep, and consistent Training (R.E.S.T.) are fundamental pillars of a stress-resilient lifestyle. Tailor these elements to fit your schedule and preferences. If that means training for 20 minutes and relaxing for 3 hours, go for it! What matters is that it works for you and helps you meet your deadlines without adding to your stress levels.

- Track your feelings.

There's a sweet spot in your stress level called the "optimal zone." In this zone, you're alert, focused, and primed to perform at your best. However, if the stress escalates and you start doubting your abilities, you've crossed over into the danger zone of supra-stress. So, the key is to recognize your emotional tipping point. Where in your body do you feel the stress build up? What negative self-talk begins? What triggers this shift? Scribble these observations down in your stress journal. Reflect on past events that might have wired these stress responses into your system. Why was this response protective in the past? Perhaps it was a coping mechanism you developed as a child feeling helpless? Now, challenge this old defense mechanism. Write down at least three reasons why this learned behavior doesn't serve you anymore. Understanding your stress response is the first step toward rewriting your stress story.

- Practice patience.

Impatience often sneaks stressors into your life, most of the time avoidable ones. For example, there are two lines at the post office, so you pick the shorter one. By Murphy's Law, the other line will move faster. So you decide to change lines. But fate chose to laugh at you that day. The line you just left becomes faster. You notice your heart pumping blood a bit more forcefully. If you had stayed in the first line, you'd already be done. Impatience can turn the simplest of tasks into stressors. It cranks up your nerves, sends your stress hormones into overdrive, and sets your heart pounding. Your mind goes into overdrive, spinning scenarios of being late while you remain stuck in line, helpless.

But here's the good news: patience is a learnable skill. You can hone your patience, transforming your relationship with stressors with practice. The result? A freer, lighter life where stressors no longer hold the reins.

So, take a deep breath, slow down, and remember - patience is power. And it's a power you can cultivate.

How can you become more patient?

First off, pinpoint the triggers that turn your cool into chaos. Are these triggers specific to people, words, behaviors, or situations like rush hour traffic? If you've already identified your stressors, it'll be easier to select those that also stir up impatience. If not, it's not too late to catch up!

The journey toward patience begins with awareness. By bringing the subconscious triggers of impatience to the conscious realm, you gain the power to control them.

Grab a piece of paper and divide it into two columns. In the first one, jot down instances from today where you lost your patience. It could be something like, "My partner was dragging a story," or "The waiter was slow to take my order." Once you have a list, try to articulate the 'why' behind your impatience for each situation. Be brutally honest with yourself. For example, "I lost patience with my partner because I was rushing, and they chose that moment to start a story," or "I became impatient with the waiter because they served people who came in after me."

Underneath every moment of impatience lies an unfulfilled need. The people or situations that trigger our impatience are just the stimuli, not the cause. They can't make us impatient unless we choose to react. There is a precious gap between stimulus and response; in this gap, we have the freedom to choose our reaction - thank you for pointing that out, Victor Frankl.

After identifying our stressors, the second step is to reframe the root of our impatience. As I mentioned, impatience arises from an unmet need. So, identify that need.

Let's take this example: "I lost my patience with my partner because I was in a rush, and they decided to tell me their story right when I was about to head out." The unmet need here is the desire for your partner to consider your time constraints. You wished they were more attentive, prioritizing your need to rush over their story, which could've been shared later. There's also a component of poor time management on your part contributing to the impatience. Perhaps you could've woken up earlier to comfortably meet your morning obligations.

If you were to voice your impatience in this situation, you might say something like, "Can't you see I'm rushing? What's the point of this story? I feel like you'll never get to the end." Confronted with this, your partner will likely go on the defensive, feeling attacked and less inclined to empathize with your needs. They might sulk or start an argument. In the end, both your needs

and showing appreciation for their work might gain their respect and cooperation.

It's time for you to think of at least three instances where you lost your patience.

-Recall your reactions and write them down.

-Recognize who or what you initially blamed for your impatience and realize that they were merely the stimulus.

-Identify the real unmet need that triggered your negative reaction and rephrase your response to focus on communicating these needs rather than blaming others.

Once you've completed this exercise, rank how seriously the situation that triggered your impatience will affect you tomorrow on a scale of one to ten. How about next week? Next year? Chances are, you'll likely have forgotten all about it by next week, let alone next year.

Remember that most perceived "offenses" are unintentional. People don't conspire to make us miserable. We just fail to identify our own unmet needs and feelings instead of finding it easier to blame others for our distress. Try to be introspective when you lose patience. If you feel the typical signs of impatience—rapid breathing and heartbeat, foggy thinking, clenched fists, agitation—take a step back. Take five to ten deep breaths, identify the unmet need behind your impatience, and rephrase your response to concentrate on that need.

For instances where your impatience is provoked by inanimate objects or situations you can't address, like a traffic jam, try this exercise: Breathe deeply, focus on something you're looking forward to or a pleasant memory from your past, and let the tension dissipate. Stay in this relaxed state as well as you can. Inform anyone who needs to know that you'll be late.

A practical patience training exercise could be raising a plant or a small tree. Start from a seed or a small root branch. Water it as needed, provide it with appropriate nutrients, and care for it. This practice can cultivate both your patience and caretaking skills.

Key takeaways to discipline your mind:

- Become aware of your stressors. Realize that the stressors are only the stimulus of your stress and impatience. You are the only one who can control the interpretation of any stressful situation.

- Behind every impatient outburst, there is an unmet need. Articulate this need and focus on it instead of culpability when you address your stressor.

Chapter 6: Be at Peace with Your Virtual Life

According to studies, people today are much less happy. Anxiety disorders, mental illness, and depression are much more common than when everything was actually more depressing – or at least, there are much more studies documenting it. We live in an epidemic of perfectionism - have the perfect body, be perfectly happy, rich, funny, smart, and witty. Be more productive, bring better results, post perfect pictures on social media about your perfectly nutritious breakfast, hop in your perfect car, and whistle happy melodies to get in perfect time to your perfect workplace. But when do we pause to ask ourselves: what exactly are we seeking?

ruin your day, obstruct your ambitions, or hinder your pursuit of a fulfilling life unless you allow them to.

• Embrace ambiguity. Worrying excessively about others' opinions can disrupt the flow of your life. Understand that people's views of you are shaped more by their personal experiences and prejudices, over which you have no control. As Queen Elsa from Frozen wisely advises, sometimes you just need to "let it go."

• Concentrate on what truly counts. Life is short. When we're preoccupied with others' opinions, we lose sight of what really matters. People will form opinions, and there's only so much you can do to alter them. Don't let this hold you back. Instead, focus on how you see yourself and allow your core beliefs and values to guide you toward a contented and purposeful life.

• Don't be ruled by fear; formulate a plan. Often, we let our imaginations run wild, expecting the worst. Yet, the worst seldom occurs; even when it does, its impact rarely lasts forever. Instead of dwelling on negative outcomes, redirect your thinking towards constructive solutions. Preparing a simple action plan for worst-case scenarios can bring perspective and alleviate fears.

• Recognize and celebrate that you are a work in progress. When confronted with the highlight reels of others' lives on social media, you have two choices: to wallow in self-doubt or see it as an opportunity for self-improvement. Remember, we're all on a growth journey, continually learning and evolving. When comparisons are inevitable, turn them into a springboard for personal growth. Adopt healthier habits, seek knowledge, immerse yourself in what you love, and live your best life. Remember, your unique journey will generate plenty of beautiful moments worth sharing.

So, put these strategies into practice and liberate yourself from the tyranny of social media anxieties. Reclaim your power, celebrate your uniqueness, and embrace the joy of living a life true to yourself.

Key takeaways to discipline your mind:

- Social media doesn't change the core of who we are, but it can certainly magnify the insecurities that exist within us. We need to be self-aware, monitor how we are affected by the opinions others share about us on social media, and recognize when it is in our best interest to take a step back and focus on getting our sense of self-worth from within.

- Recognize that little on social media is exactly as it seems. Don't be so hard on yourself by unfairly comparing the ordinary moments of your life with the "best moments" people choose to display on social media. Understand that everyone has ordinary moments, just like you, and you should not feel inferior.

- Realize that everyone has their own problems and challenges to deal with, which means they aren't thinking about and judging you nearly as much as you believe they are. Spend more of your time and attention on the things that really matter – improving yourself, developing your own identity and feeling of self-worth from within, and living your best life instead of worrying so much about the opinions of others.

ago, my answer to who I was and my life's purpose revolved around my boyfriend and our shared dream of raising chickens on a farm. Today, that answer feels almost laughable. And that's okay.

Psychologists have found that the narratives we spin about ourselves seriously influence our actions positively and negatively. If you see yourself as smart, you're likely to perform better in cognitive tasks, tests, and debates. Our beliefs have power over us. This is precisely the reason why we should be aware of them and learn to question them over time.

The Zen Buddhist philosophy identifies two types of mind: the thinking mind and the observing mind. The thinking mind is the incessant chatterbox inside your head. Even during meditation, it continues to spawn thoughts and images. It's always at work - while you're waiting in a queue, about to sleep, and sometimes even during sleep. Have you ever noticed this internal chatter? Yes? Then you did it with your observing mind.

The observing mind is the silent spectator that keeps tabs on your thoughts and actions. Unfortunately, we often underutilize this facet of our mind.

Before diving into Zen Buddhism, I was unaware of this distinction. I used to label my observing mind as my 'better judgment' or 'right mind,' and when my thoughts ran rampant, I felt 'out of my mind.' So, when someone exclaims, "What were you thinking? You're not in your right mind!" they're really saying, "Hey, your thinking mind seems to be running amok. Time to engage your observing mind!"

When the thinking mind gets out of control, the observing mind can't do much about it. Have you ever asked someone for help on how to channel your anger? "What can I do to stop feeling anger?"

The answer is once the thinking mind unleashes anger, it's like a wild horse bolting out of the stable. However, it's important to remember that you can't and shouldn't try to suppress your emotions. The key is not to get entangled in them.

What you can do is not identify with your emotions. Zen teaches that instead of telling yourself, "I am angry," say, "I feel anger." This slight shift in perspective helps you acknowledge that you are not the human form of anger. You are just experiencing this emotion. By the way, you can separate yourself from the emotion and give yourself space to accept, embrace, and dissolve it.[xvii]

Remember, emotions sprout from your subconscious and are beyond your control, but how you react to them is in your hands. As soon as you realize your thinking mind is spinning into chaos, catch yourself in that moment. Acknowledge and accept that you feel anger, fear, or anxiety, and consciously take them under your mental microscope.

Emotions like anger and impatience often stem from unmet needs, either yours or someone else's. Suppose you're trying to communicate with your partner, who seems distant. Frustrated, you might think, "Talking to him is like talking to a statue." However, if you look at your feelings closely, you'll realize your anger is a smokescreen for your real need - to be heard and understood.[xviii] When you communicate your needs more authentically, instead of lashing out with, "You're like a statue; it's impossible to talk to you," try expressing, "I don't feel heard right now. I need to feel connected and understood."

Similarly, if someone vents their anger at you or something you're passionate about, try to uncover the unmet need fueling their hostility. Let's say your partner accuses you of being emotionally constipated. Here, you have several options: you can criticize yourself for being impassive, harbor resentment towards your partner for the harsh comment, or introspect on your feelings and seek the unmet need behind their anger.

Your partner's comment might sting because you feel your efforts to be expressive are unnoticed. Simultaneously, your partner might be lashing out due to their need for more emotional engagement. Instead of retorting angrily, "You are such a jerk, and what you said is very unfair," you could respond, "Thank you for your honesty. I understand that you need more emotional feedback from me. However, your comment made me feel unappreciated and upset because I do try to express myself."

Remember, you may not have control over experiencing anger, but you do have control over how you express it. Marshall B. Rosenberg's book,

Nonviolent Communication, provides invaluable insights into the peaceful communication of negative emotions. It's highly recommended if you want to delve deeper into this topic.

Separate your emotions from your identity. You are not your emotions. The more you choose to focus on your emotions, the more powerful they become. Even if you focus on getting rid of negative emotions, you're still operating from the framework of the negative. Focusing on something you don't want to do is much less effective than focusing your attention on the things you want to do. For example, instead of saying, "I don't want to feel anger," say, "I want to feel peaceful."

Embrace that negative thoughts and emotions are part of life. You can't get rid of them, but you can let them go. Reframe negative statements like "I hate my job" to "I'm feeling hatred towards my job." Doing so creates a mental and verbal distance from the issue, allowing you to see these negative emotions as transient states, not unchangeable facts.

Self-discipline

Research reveals that individuals with heightened self-discipline tend to be happier and capable of navigating challenging situations with grace and optimism. Crisis periods are shorter in their lives, and they can make positive decisions more easily and rationally.

Like patience, self-discipline isn't an inborn trait but an acquired skill. It doesn't come naturally, but this quality can be honed with perseverance and focused effort, promising to enrich long-term dividends. With self-discipline, you're better positioned to make enlightened, healthier choices and exercise control over your emotions, leading to more balanced and less impulsive decisions.

What's the difference between patience and self-discipline?

Consider this simple anecdote to distinguish between patience and self-discipline. Let's take Mark, who's awaiting his tardy friends. An understanding and patient individual, Mark doesn't make a fuss about their delay. However, the array of candies and sandwiches on his table tempts him, and he ends up overeating, despite his weight issue. Mark had developed the quality of patience, so he didn't argue with his friends for being late. But he couldn't stop eating even though he wasn't that hungry. He lacked self-control, which is the foundation of self-discipline.

An effective way to kickstart your journey towards self-discipline is by practicing the "out of sight, out of mind" principle. Self-discipline is about acknowledging your temptations and refusing their control over you, be it a bad eating habit or the irresistible urge to check your phone amidst a crucial task.

With self-discipline, your conscious mind grows robust enough to resist these temptations, even when they stare right at you. As a starting point, I'd recommend eliminating these triggers from your immediate surroundings.

Consider Mia's case. She decided to tackle her weight issue through a strict diet, consuming only a single low-carb meal and protein shakes daily. Despite feeling proud of her newfound self-discipline, she became increasingly irritable, struggled with concentration, and essentially lost control of everything but her diet.

Maintaining self-discipline becomes challenging when your fundamental needs - akin to the base of Maslow's pyramid - aren't met. [xix] Strike a balance in your eating, drinking, and sleeping habits to support your discipline. Ensure you're fueling your brain adequately; regulated blood sugar levels foster better focus and productivity.

Remember, comfort isn't the end goal. Embracing self-discipline to break free from ingrained habits often stirs discomfort, a natural brain response favoring the status quo. The brain doesn't like changes, the comfort zone is its normal state, and the brain tries to eliminate everything that threatens this comfort. Yet, if you persist with discipline, your brain will gradually adapt to the new habits, constructing a fresh comfort zone.

Habit formation is neither quick nor easy. On your journey towards disciplined living, expect to stumble and falter. Forgive yourself and remember, self-discipline isn't about morphing into a paragon of perfection but about gaining clarity on who you are, what your limitations are, where you need to improve, assuming control over your life, and picking your battles wisely.

Self-awareness begins when you learn to say 'no' to others, but self-discipline kicks off when you learn to say 'no' to yourself. Ready to conquer your goals? Shed the cloak of excuses, stride onto your chosen path today, and vow to stay committed, come what may!

"Discipline is the bridge between goals and accomplishment."

- Jim Rohn

Key takeaways to discipline your mind:

- Learn to be patient. Notice the unmet needs behind your anger or the anger of someone else. Focus on addressing these needs instead of blaming yourself or others.

- Cultivate self-discipline. Keep your basic needs satisfied (eat well, drink, and sleep enough) so you won't sabotage your discipline and focus.

Chapter 8: Pay Attention to What Thoughts You Feed

Have you ever wanted something badly, and somehow you got it but didn't understand how? The only explanation you could find was that you "attracted" it with the power of your thoughts.

The human mind is truly tremendous. It has the power to create the greatest companies in the world, but it can also be used to destroy. Whatever you think about creates your reality. That's why I always warn myself, "Be careful of what you think because one day it may come true."

The things you experience in the outside world have their origin in your inner world. In other words, your reactions to your circumstances result from your beliefs, attitudes, and habits. Your thoughts affect the state of your health, relationships, and finances.

If you don't like what you see or experience, it's time to change the lenses through which you look at the world. People think their life will also change if they change something external. But a new house, car, phone, or hairstyle rarely brings meaningful changes to the soul. True change happens inside the head, not on the outside.

How to Switch on the Power of Conscious Thinking?

Throughout our day-to-day life, most of us are consumed by activities without paying much attention to our thoughts. Have you ever examined how your mind operates? Are you aware of what triggers fear within you or what mental dialogues you have with yourself throughout the day? We carry on with our routines - eat, work, socialize, make plans, have fun, and engage with others - but rarely do we consciously inhabit these moments.

Meditation and silent introspection practiced for a few minutes a day can bring life-changing miracles. Engage actively with your thoughts and actions - when you're about to grab a cold drink from the kitchen or feeling frustrated about a delayed payment at work. Tune into your thoughts and emotions in relation to ordinary, everyday events, just as you do with significant ones.

Remember, what you feed your mind, you empower and eventually attract. While the whole concept of the law of attraction can be debated, its effects can sometimes manifest in surprising or inexplicable ways.

What we call the law of attraction has more to do with self-awareness. When we're engulfed in negativity, we tend to miss out on the world around us. We're so absorbed in our troubles that we overlook opportunities that come our way. And hence, with a clouded mindset, we don't "attract" anything positive because our minds are closed.

Conversely, when we're carefree, living in the moment, and filled with hope, we often stumble upon lucky finds. We notice that job opening, enter that competition, and meet amazing people. We invite positivity into our lives by simply being open, engaged, and kind.

I have a friend who's an ardent believer in the law of attraction. He's read all of Rhonda Byrne's books and diligently practices the principles, but I believe he's misunderstood the concept. His recent hobby is to "attract" buses. Thanks to him and his bus-manifesting Jedi mind trick, I became a writer. You heard it right!

Years ago, while we were heading somewhere, he abruptly stopped, closed his eyes, and focused intensely - as if "attracting" a bus with the force of his mind. Back then, I wasn't into self-help, and I was quite skeptical. You can imagine my disbelief and bewilderment, especially after I made sure he actually meant what he said. I took a deep breath to swallow my sarcasm and patiently waited for the bus that showed up a few minutes later. ("Your negative thoughts chased it away. That's why we had to wait for so long," was his explanation.)

My friend achieved one thing, though. Even if he didn't teleport a bus for us in the next thirty seconds, this bizarre incident sparked my curiosity about the concept that strongly influenced my friend. It led me to purchase my first self-help book, 'The Secret.' On reflection, his "bus attraction" practice indirectly inspired me to explore this genre and eventually pen down my thoughts in this book. Did I always want to become a writer? Was this a grand design of the universe, unknowingly guiding me toward my goal?

Or was it more about me taking an interest in a new topic, learning, and gradually compiling my thoughts into this self-help book? Well, that's a question I'll leave for you to ponder.

"Weak is he who permits his thoughts to control his actions; strong is he who forces his actions to control his thoughts."
   - Og Mandino

Your brain is wired to focus on only one thing at a time. Let that single point of focus be something positive and constructive. To bring about a transformation in your external circumstances, you need to first alter your internal mindset. Nurture your conscious mind to remain open and success-focused rather than dwelling on negatives. Keep your mind occupied with hopeful expectations and take action in line with them. You'll soon discover that you're drawing the things you desire towards yourself, not due to any mystical cosmic force, but through your own efforts.

Learning to act in your best interest doesn't require you to whisper spells to attract positive results. The one thing you should believe is that you are deserving of whatever you're striving to attain. This doesn't mean feeling a sense of entitlement. Rather it's about perceiving yourself as worthy of your desires.

Why is this important? If you feel unworthy of something, you won't be able to act in your best interest to get it. You may feel that what you desire is too good or too challenging for you to obtain. Consequently, the "Universe" won't grant you your desire because you've essentially given up on persistently pursuing it.

Let's say you're aspiring for a role in design, and you believe you're deserving of it. What would you do? You'd refine your resume, promote yourself unabashedly, share your work samples with a wide array of companies - big and small, and consistently enhance your design skills. Then, on a seemingly ordinary Friday morning, you might receive an interview call from a prestigious company. Was it the Universe's doing? Indeed, because you expanded your opportunities and cast your net wide in the Universe. You acted in your best interest, and the Universe responded.

Add to your attraction some constructive actions. It's like playing the lottery - you first need to buy a ticket to stand a chance of winning. There's a Hungarian saying, "Help yourself, and God will help you, too." This proverb perfectly encapsulates the essence of the law of attraction - just replace 'God' with 'the Universe.'

Key takeaway to discipline your mind:

- Believe first and foremost in your efforts. Whatever you wish to get in life, you have a better chance of getting it if you walk around with an open mind. Take steps that help you to get closer to your wish; don't attract, act.

Chapter 9: Failing and Learning

Once upon a time, a young man ran away from his family at an early age, fudged his age to become an ambulance driver, was sacked from a newspaper job due to his supposed lack of creativity, failed at launching a cartoon series in Kansas City, and started several other unsuccessful businesses. One day, this man drew an intriguing mouse character that was dismissed for being too frightening. He also suffered the tragic loss of his mother in a carbon dioxide accident in a house he built her in hopes of providing her with a better life. His staff abandoned him to fight in World War II, leading him to convert his studio into a tank repair artillery. This man was drowning in a four-million-dollar debt, struggling to open his first amusement park for families. This man was none other than Walt Disney - a name synonymous with pinnacle success today.xx

No matter how disciplined, focused, or optimistic we are, life throws curveballs at us. Failure and adversity sneak into our lives regardless of our best efforts. It's important to understand that failure isn't a sign of defeat; it's an inherent part of life's journey.

Indeed, failure often proves to be life's best teacher. Authentic growth blossoms from a myriad of minor and major setbacks. If you admire someone for their mastery in a particular area, rest assured they've weathered their share of failures to reach their current skill level.

When you learned to talk, you mispronounced some words, babbled, and sometimes confused words and meanings. Still, you didn't give up until you learned to talk. As a child, you never thought that maybe talking wasn't for you and never said a word again.

Ironically, many of our failures stem from unrealistic standards we set for ourselves. The aspiration to "be the smartest in my team" places you in a precarious position where control eludes you. You can't influence how much your team members study or how naturally gifted they are at presenting (remember your Circle of Influence). This pursuit will leave you perpetually anxious, constantly in combat with the world, and reliant on others. You've set a challenging benchmark for yourself. Conversely, if your objective is to "improve my presentation skills from adequate to great," you'll meet your goal regardless of your colleagues' performance. You are in the driver's seat.

Establish standards that fall within your Circle of Influence to avoid unnecessary failures.

Failure universally evokes feelings of loss, anxiety, and sorrow. However, the duration it takes each individual to recover from these negative emotions varies. Some of us possess an uncanny ability to bounce back from failures almost instantly, flashing a smile the next day. Others may brood over their setback for weeks, ruminating on what went wrong. There are those who talk incessantly about their failures, while some prefer silence and feign indifference. Attempts to offer help to some may even be met with anger.

Generally, it's vital not to internalize failures. A single setback doesn't label you as a failure. On the contrary, failure and heartbreak arm you with invaluable wisdom and experience. That said, it's crucial to understand why you failed so that you can extract lessons that will contribute to your personal growth. Failure without learning is merely pointless suffering.

Ask yourself these questions:

- Why triggered my failure?

- What actions might have brought about a better outcome?
- Was the failure completely beyond my control?
- After gathering the facts, take a step back and ask: what did I learn from this?

Sometimes, our concern isn't so much about the failure itself but rather the potential criticism from others. Don't let this burden you. Those who judge you based on your missteps aren't worth your energy. Don't try to conceal your failures. Embracing and acknowledging a setback, adversity, or flaw can often garner you more respect than attempting to obscure it.

Success never comes without a price. Yet, the sweetness of success is all the more pronounced when we finally achieve what we want against all odds. Thus, welcome failure, reconcile with it and use it as a stepping stone towards personal growth.

Find peace with your past failures if they continue to linger in your mind. Visit a place where you once experienced a significant failure. It could be your former school, your previous workplace, or any place that resonates. I personally revisited a specific table in a Burger King restaurant where I had my first heartbreak – where my first boyfriend broke up with me. It felt like my world had crumbled at the time, and I believed I would never recover.

For several years, I steered clear of that place. But one day, I gathered the courage to return. I bought a burger and sat at the dreaded table. I had expected an overwhelming wave of catharsis, but instead, I felt nothing. I had long moved on, yet I kept nursing the pain, thinking it would still sting if I confronted it. Revisiting the place and experiencing nothing reaffirmed my healing and underscored the need to "test" reality.

Confronting a location that was once the epicenter of a traumatic experience can be surprisingly sobering. Finding no remaining trace of your past pain, humiliation, or disappointment allows healing to seep in. To truly let go of the past, write down every sorrowful, infuriating, unfair, painful feeling and thought associated with that location. Tear up the paper, burn it if it is possible safely, bury it, pelt stones at it, and do anything that helps release any lingering tension.

Once you've done this, walk away.

What past baggage are you clinging onto that's impeding your progress? Did certain individuals negatively impact you? Were you hurt, deceived, or mistreated by someone? Did you inflict these actions on someone else? Are you grappling with feelings of frustration?

What's the first step you need to take to let it go?

Let your tears flow - unabashedly and audibly. Suppressing your emotions can lead to physical illness. Instead, direct your attention to the present, allowing you to grasp the reality of your current situation.

Do you feel anger? Don't try to avoid this feeling; rather, feel it fully. Allow it some space, sit with it, and consciously stop reacting to it. Just feel it; allow it to burn down in you. Breathe. Emotions last only a couple of minutes, and if you don't keep them up with thoughts, they leave your system. Nothing lasts forever, and neither will anger.

Are past relationships anchoring you down? Quit idolizing the bond and confront the truth. Objectively list out the positives and negatives you experienced in this relationship. This exercise may assist you in realizing that the negatives may outweigh the positives, which likely precipitated the end of the relationship.

Remember, there will always be individuals who align better with us than the people who choose to leave us. Avoid the trap of believing that no one will ever love you as much as they did. Strive to love yourself to the maximum. Once you master self-love, the need for emotional validation from others will significantly diminish.

Know that the sun will always come out when the rain is over. If you know that something good will follow, you'll let go much easier.

My father shared a poignant tale when I was heartbroken. In ancient India, a young girl requested her father for a birthday gift that could uplift her spirits in gloomy times and ground her when she's flying too high. Acknowledging her wish, the father gifted her a medallion on her birthday with a profound four-worded inscription: "This too shall pass."

Key takeaway to discipline your mind:

- When you fail, don't hide from it. Accept it and allow yourself to feel the pain. Then talk about it, stop romanticizing it, and harness the lessons you can learn from it. Remember, neither pain nor success will last forever.

Chapter 10: Practice, Practice, Practice

The adage goes, "Practice makes perfect." As Thomas M. Sterner, the author of 'The Practicing Mind,' rightly pointed out, "Life itself is one long practice session. Everything in life worth achieving requires practice." [xxi]

When we bring up the concept of practice, it often conjures images of practicing a sport or a musical instrument. But countless other facets of life require practice, like cultivating patience, enhancing communication skills, or embracing the habit of meditation. Sterner suggests that the true objective should be sustaining the practice process rather than concentrating on the result. According to him, being process-oriented and present cultivates self-discipline, acute focus, patience, and self-awareness.

When my mother married my father, she discovered that she had a daunting task ahead. My father was a huge fan of his mother's cooking, and my mother had to prove that she could cook just as well. This seems like a simple problem to solve, right?

In her quest to recreate my father's favorite home-cooked meals, my mother turned to my grandmother for her treasured recipes – especially her renowned oyster dressing recipe she prepared every Thanksgiving. But here lay the problem, my grandmother believed in cooking by "feel" and never wrote down any recipes.

To master the elusive oyster dressing, my mother shadowed my grandmother in the kitchen, observing her every move and noting down her instructions. However, this was more challenging than anticipated as my grandmother never measured her ingredients and often advised her to add "a pinch" of this or that.

Through countless Thanksgivings and persistent practice, my mother finally nailed the recipe, much to her own and my father's delight. This recipe now serves as a testament to my mother's tenacity and the culinary prowess of both my grandmother and mother.

It's easy to fall into the trap of believing that only creative pursuits or work-related activities necessitate practice. Yet, all areas we wish to improve in our lives demand practice, whether it's parenting, learning to budget, or planning the ideal vacation.

Seems daunting, doesn't it? It appears as though every single moment of our twenty-four-hour day is a practice session. Well, yes and no. There's a strategic element to this equation, and that is prioritizing. Decide on the areas (goals) where you desire to reap significant rewards for your strenuous efforts, roll up your sleeves, and consistently work towards these objectives.

The difference between practice and learning

It's common for people to equate 'practicing' with 'learning,' seeing them as interchangeable concepts. Yet, Thomas Sterner, the author of 'The Practicing Mind,' elucidates that 'practice' and 'learning' are distinctly separate. He asserts that "practice" suggests an awareness and will that the term 'learning' doesn't necessarily encapsulate. [xxii]

The act of 'practicing' something is intentional. We consciously repeat a task to attain a specific goal. This repetitive action fosters understanding and knowledge acquisition, suggesting that learning is inherently a part of practice. However, the reverse doesn't hold true; learning doesn't inherently involve practice. When you choose to practice something, you are fully immersed in the present moment, within the motion itself.

A perfect example of this is Arnold Schwarzenegger's approach to weight training, as described in his book 'Total Recall.' He viewed his training sessions as a form of meditation, where he was mentally in tune with his muscles, sensing their tension, observing their flex, conversing with them, and commanding them to grow.[xxiii] His focus, presence, and practice were all channeled toward this singular activity. There was no self-judgment, merely the execution of an activity, the observation of results, and the subsequent adaptation to optimize future practices and attain his goal.

While it's crucial not to let the result be your sole objective, you can harness it as a stimulus to bolster your practice. Resist the temptation to view your goal as a gauge of success or a measure of your self-worth. Instead, concentrate on mastering your own capabilities through diligent practice, always striving to perform your best in the present moment. When you stay focused and productive, you'll experience a sense of contentment at day's end, even if your goal hasn't been reached. However, if you surrender to distractions and procrastination, even if you manage to complete your day's objectives, you'll find yourself with an unshakeable feeling of incompleteness. This void emanates from not being the best version of yourself that you could be.

The disciplined mind rejects instant gratification

Why do we procrastinate if we know and feel – consciously and subconsciously - that it is bad for us? Because in the heat of the moment, the pain of doing what we should seems greater than doing nothing. In other words, we choose instant gratification, a short-term satisfaction that never has lasting value.

However, through mindful practice, you can learn to resist the allure of transient pleasures. Pause and reflect on your past – how many significant achievements can you recount that required little or no effort on your part? Now try to recall those accomplishments for which you toiled persistently and patiently over an extended duration. Were these hard-earned victories more valuable to you? The sense of elation and fulfillment that you derive from the fruits of your efforts and struggles is incomparable to any quick and effortless gain.

A disciplined mind notices when it falls out of the present moment

Have you ever dipped your toes into the serene waters of meditation? If so, you'd know that its goal isn't to wrestle your mind into complete silence but rather to guide your focus gently toward the present moment. Yes, your mind will undoubtedly be visited by an army of thoughts –

but that's perfectly okay! Meditation isn't a quest to achieve a thoughtless state; it's a journey of acknowledging those thoughts and then gently nudging your attention back to the present – usually your breath.

If you practice meditation enough, your mind starts to develop a sharp awareness of the thoughts and emotions that ripple across your consciousness throughout the day. Whether it's impatience, anger, boredom, sadness, self-disappointment, or any other emotion, you'll be able to bring awareness to these feelings. And you'll notice something fascinating – these emotions are rarely about the present moment. Apprehensions about the future or regrets from the past often fuel them. This realization means that whenever you detect these negative feelings stirring, it's a sign that your mind has strayed away from the present. Take note of where your focus has wandered. Acknowledge the unwelcome guest – whether it's fear, anxiety, or anger – with a simple, "Hello, I see you. Come, sit with me for a while, and then you may leave." Then, take a few soothing deep breaths, and gently guide your focus back to the present moment.'

When you are practicing something, it's only worth doing if you are in the here and now. That's when and where the knowledge absorbs. That's how you get the greatest return on your time investment. When you are practicing well, you are not aware you are practicing well.

Mastering the art of present-moment awareness is a lifelong journey. It's not a badge of honor to flaunt or a skill to list on your resume under the title "Expert in staying present." Rather, it's a powerful tool to infuse your life with a sense of tranquility and inner peace that nothing else can quite offer. So, step into this journey and let the present moment's richness unravel for you.

Don't look for shortcuts.

Attempting to cheat discipline is a futile endeavor. It's a strategy that will neither serve you in the short run nor in the long haul. There's no shortcut, no hack that will lead you to mastery. To echo Jim Rohn, "You can't hire someone else to do your push-ups for you."

Unfortunately, many shy away from hard work, fleeing the discomfort it induces. Others see the toll of hard work as an unwelcome nuisance. Some even take pride in their ability to find the shortest path to their objectives, viewing it as resourcefulness. This approach may work when it comes to navigating through traffic or wrapping up a project swiftly. However, when the goal is personal growth or the adoption of healthier habits, shortcuts become acts of self-sabotage.

It's common for individuals to focus on the final objective—the outcome they desire from their efforts. Ironically, this outcome often brings the least amount of satisfaction in the entire journey. Reflect upon your past experiences. When you succeeded after a prolonged struggle, was it the climax that brought you the most joy? Or did you derive more pleasure from successfully navigating a challenging day or finding your newly acquired skills useful in day-to-day life? The beauty of life lies in the journey, not the destination.

So, fall in love with the journey. Embrace the process, knowing that each day of dedicated practice moves you closer to your objective. No goal will feel too immense or daunting when you learn to derive pleasure from the journey. You can progress steadily without being overwhelmed by breaking down your big goal into manageable daily tasks. As long as you remain within the process, each day will bring its own sense of satisfaction.

Key takeaways to discipline your mind:

- Practice is not simply for artistic and athletic endeavors. Everything worth achieving in life takes practice.

- The best practice occurs when you are present at the moment and completely focused on the task at hand. When our mind is disciplined, we are willing to delay gratification to work toward achieving something truly meaningful rather than getting sidetracked by the distraction of instant gratification that will offer little value to our lives in the long term.

- We can intentionally create the habits we want in our lives by being aware of the goal we want to achieve, breaking it down into steps that will require our repetitive practice and focus, and performing those steps repeatedly without judgment until they become second nature to us.

Closing Thoughts

Disciplining the mind is not something that comes easily or naturally to us. Our minds are chatty, buzzing, and active all the time. Even advanced meditators can't shut their minds off completely. They are just good at letting go of their thoughts and jumping back to the present moment. However, attempting to make our minds a bit more disciplined pays off even if we can't do it perfectly.

Here are a few of the benefits that come from having a disciplined mind:

- You become keenly aware of the things that are within and beyond your control. You accept responsibility for where you are in your life and your response to what

146

happens to you. You do not waste precious time trying to place blame or waiting for someone else to rescue you and improve your life for you. You understand that meaningful and lasting change comes from within.

- You approach your life with your eyes wide open. You recognize that everything in life is a tradeoff and that when you choose to pursue one goal or focus on one area of your life, there will be a cost in that you are unable to devote your time and energy to other areas. You understand that it is possible to have it all – just not all at the same time. You set your priorities and maintain your focus on achieving your goals.

- You recognize that stress and negative emotions are not something you can avoid or banish from your life. They are inevitable, and everyone experiences them. But you understand that you have the power to control the way you respond to them. You know that stress and negative feelings are really a manifestation of needs that aren't being met, and you are willing to put in the time and effort to discover what those unmet needs are and find a healthy way to address them.

- You work to overcome temptations and are able to forego instant gratification in favor of more meaningful and valuable delayed gratification. You keep your eye on the prize and maintain your focus and effort in trying to reach your long-term goals without getting distracted and allowing your progress to get derailed.

- You accept that you are a work in progress. You know you will make mistakes and fail at times in your life, but you don't let it get you down, and you aren't too hard on yourself because you know it's all a part of the learning and growing process we call life.

In order to have a more disciplined mind, try to keep the following tips in mind:

- Try not to worry too much about what others think of you. They are too busy worrying about their own problems and challenges to judge you as much as you think they are. Remember that your identity and feeling of self-worth should come from within, not from the opinions of others.

- Always be willing to challenge and re-evaluate your beliefs to make sure that they still fit you today. Speak to people with differing viewpoints and do some research to make sure that they aren't negative and outdated. If you are presented with facts or evidence that warrants it, be willing to adapt or discard them instead of just clinging to them because they are comforting.

- Approach social media in moderation. Be self-aware and know when you are taking the opinions of others too much to heart. Be willing to step away when it takes up too much of your time and energy or negatively affects your self-confidence.

- Find your passion and purpose in life and pursue it with abandon.

- Don't be afraid to fail. Failure is a necessary part of life because it teaches us some of the best lessons and enables us to grow. Accept it and learn from it as you continuously try to improve yourself.

- Live in the present. Focus your mind and practice, practice, practice. Everything worth achieving in life requires it.

Thank you for choosing this book to read and for making me a small part of your self-improvement journey on your quest to develop a more disciplined mind. I wish for you a chance to live your best life. Start moving today in the direction of your dreams, knowing that you are now equipped with some additional strategies and the power within you to create the life you want for yourself. Accept responsibility for your own happiness and start taking action right away.

I believe in you!

Zoe

One Last Thing...

Maybe you don't realize it, but you have unlimited power in the arena of authors and readers. You're Julius Caesar in the Colosseum and I'm the gladiator anxiously waiting for your thumbs shifting up or down. If your thumb goes up, it's amazing! I feel validated, happy, and enabled to prepare myself for another book-battle. If your thumb goes down, and you tell me why, that's great too – I can learn, grow, and find ways to serve you better in the future.

Independent authors like myself depend on your, the reader's, feedback. With no publishing behemoth behind us, we need to invest our hard-earned 9-5 job money and free time into honing our passion, writing. Your feedback about your reading experience is vital for other readers to know about this book.

How did you like How to Discipline Your Mind? If you feel this book helped you in any way, gave you some insights, or simply entertained you it would mean a lot if you could:

1.   Please leave a review on Amazon, or…

2.   Please leave a review on goodreads.com. Here is a link to my profile where you find all my books.

https://www.goodreads.com/author/show/1496754 2.Zoe_McKey , or…

3.   Send me a private message to zoemckey@gmail.com, and

4.   Tell your friends and family about your reading experience.

Thank you so much for choosing to read my book among the many out there.

If you'd like to receive an update once I have a new book, you can subscribe to my newsletter at www.zoemckey.com. You'll get my Self-Discovery Starter Kit for FREE and a few surprise bonuses. You'll also get occasional book recommendations from other authors I trust and know they deliver good quality books.

Other Books by Zoe

"The more that you read, the more things you will know. The more that you learn, the more places you'll go."
-Dr. Seuss.

Don't stop the learning train. Check out my other titles.

Brave Enough

Time to learn how to overcome the feeling of inferiority and achieve success. Brave Enough takes you step by step through the process of understanding the nature of your fears, overcome limiting beliefs and gain confidence with the help of studies, personal stories and actionable exercises at the end of each chapter.

Say goodbye to fear of rejection and inferiority complex once and for all.

How to Be Whole Again

Did you have emotionally immature, selfish, distant parents or partners? Is their painful heritage still lingering in the form of abandonment issues, anxiety, or anger? Were your emotional needs often unmet, your opinion and emotions dismissed?

In this essential book, bestselling author and former confidence coach, Zoe McKey, exposes the harmful consequences emotional unavailability and toxic relationships can have. Experiences with such people create a feeling of neglect, inadequacy, or unworthiness. Find ways to heal from the pain.

Less Mess Less Stress

Don't compromise with your happiness. "Good enough" is not the life you deserve - you deserve the best, and the good news is that you can have it. Learn the surprising truth that it's not by doing more, but less with Less Mess Less Stress.

We know that we own too much, we say yes for too many engagements, and we stick to more than we should. Physical, mental and relationship clutter are daily burdens we have to deal with. Change your mindset and live a happier life with less.

Minimalist Budget

Minimalist Budget will help you to turn your bloated expenses into a well-toned budget, spending on exactly what you need and nothing else.

This book presents solutions for two major problems in our consumer society: (1) how to downsize your cravings without having to sacrifice the fun stuff, and (2) how to whip your finances into shape and follow a personalized budget.

Rewire Your Habits

Rewire Your Habits discusses which habits one should adopt to make changes in 5 life areas: self-improvement, relationships, money management, health, and free time. The book addresses every goal-setting, habit building challenge in these areas and breaks them down with simplicity and ease.

Tame Your Emotions

Tame Your Emotions is a collection of the most common and painful emotional insecurities and their antidotes. Even the most successful people have fears and self-sabotaging habits. But they also know how to use them to their advantage and keep their fears on a short leash. This is exactly what my book will teach you – using the tactics of experts and research-proven methods.

Emotions can't be eradicated. But they can be controlled.

The Art of Minimalism

The Art of Minimalism will present you 4 minimalist techniques, the bests from around the world, to give you a perspective on how to declutter your house, your mind, and your life in general. Learn how to let go of everything that is not important in your life and find methods that give you a peace of mind and happiness instead.

Keep balance at the edge of minimalism and consumerism.

The Critical Mind

If you want to become a critical, effective, and rational thinker instead of an irrational and snap-judging one, this book is for you. Critical thinking skills strengthen your decision making muscle, speed up your analysis and judgment, and help you spot errors easily.

The Critical Mind offers a thorough introduction to the rules and principles of critical thinking. You will find widely usable and situation-specific advice on how to critically approach your daily life, business, friendships, opinions, and even social media.

The Disciplined Mind

Where you end up in life is determined by a number of times you fall and get up, and how much pain and discomfort you can withstand along the way. The path to an extraordinary accomplishment and a life worth living is not innate talent, but focus, willpower, and disciplined action.

Maximize your brain power and keep in control of your thoughts.

In The Disciplined Mind, you will find unique lessons through which you will learn those essential steps and qualities that are needed to reach your goals easier and faster.

The Mind-Changing Habit of Journaling

Understand where your negative self-image, bad habits, and unhealthy thoughts come from. Know yourself to change yourself. Embrace the life-changing transformation potential of journaling. This book shows you how to use the ultimate self-healing tool of journaling to find your own answers to your most pressing problems, discover your true self and lead a life of growth mindset.

Stretch Your Mind

This book collects all the tips, tricks and tactics of the most successful people to develop your inner smartness.

Stretch Your Mind will show you how to think smarter and find your inner genius. This book is a collection of research and scientific studies about better decision-making, fairer judgments, and intuition improvement. It takes a critical look at our everyday cognitive habits and points out small but serious mistakes that are easily correctable.

Who You Were Meant To Be

Discover the strengths of your personality and how to use them to make better life choices. In Who You Were Born To Be, you'll learn some of the most influential personality-related studies. Thanks to these studies you'll learn to capitalize on your strengths, and how you can you become the best version of yourself.

Wired For Confidence

Do you feel like you just aren't good enough? End this vicious thought cycle NOW. Wired For Confidence tells you the necessary steps to break out from the pits of low self-esteem, lowered expectations, and lack of assertiveness. Take the first step to creating the life you only dared to dream of.

Reference

Boyd, John. Zimbardo, Philip. *The Time Paradox: Using the New Psychology of Time to Your Advantage.* Atria Books. 2008.

Cicchetti, D., Walker, E. Editorial: Stress and development: Biological and psychological consequences. Development and Psychopathology, 13(3), 413-418. 2001.

Crowther, Bosley. Walt Disney. Encyclopedia Britannica. 2018. https://www.britannica.com/biography/Walt-Disney

Goleman, Daniel. *Emotional Intelligence.* London: Bloomsbury. 2010

Harvard Health Publishing. Understanding the stress response. Harvard Health Publishing. 2018. https://www.health.harvard.edu/staying-healthy/understanding-the-stress-response

Liden, Matt. 8 Buddhist Tips For Dealing With Anger. Study Buddhism. 2018. https://studybuddhism.com/en/essentials/how-to/8-buddhist-tips-for-dealing-with-anger

Manson, Mark. No, You Can't Have It All. Mark Manson. 2014. https://markmanson.net/you-cant-have-it-all

Manson, Mark. *The subtle art of not giving a f*ck.* Strawberry Hills, NSW: ReadHowYouWant, 2017.

Maslow, A. H. (1943). A theory of human motivation. Psychological Review, 50(4), 370-396. http://dx.doi.org/10.1037/h0054346

Mehrabian, Albert. Albert Mehrabian Communication Studies. IOJT. 2013. http://www.iojt-dc2013.org/~/media/Microsites/Files/IOJT/110420 13-Albert-Mehrabian-Communication-Studies.ashx

Pease, Allan. Pease, Barbara. *The Definitive Book of Body Language: The Hidden Meaning Behind People's Gestures and Expressions*. Bantam. 2006.

Pressfield, Steven. The Art of War. Black Irish Entertainment LLC. 2002.

Robinson, Lawrence. Smith, Melinda. Segal, Robert. Stress Management. Helpfulguide. 2018. https://www.helpguide.org/articles/stress/stress-management.htm

Rook, K. S. (1984). The negative side of social interaction: Impact on psychological well-being.

Journal of Personality and Social Psychology, 46(5), 1097-1108. http://dx.doi.org/10.1037/0022-3514.46.5.1097

Rosenberg, Marshall B. PhD. Nonviolent Communication. PuddleDancer Press; Third Edition. 2015.

Squier, Chemmie. Why Do We Get So Obsessed With 'Likes' On Social Media? Grazia Daily. 2016. https://graziadaily.co.uk/life/opinion/care-likes-social-media/

Schwarzenegger, Arnold. Total Recall. Simon&Schuster. 2013.

Thoits, Peggy A. "Stress, Coping, and Social Support Processes: Where Are We? What Next?" Journal of Health and Social Behavior, 1995, 53-79. http://www.jstor.org/stable/2626957

Sterner, Thomas M. The Practicing Mind. New World Library. 2012.

Endnotes

[i] Covey, Stephen. Seven Habits of Highly Effective People. https://blog.hubspot.com/sales/habits-of-highly-effective-people-summary

[ii] Sivers, Derek. Don't be a donkey. Derek Siver. 2011. https://sivers.org/donkey

[iii] https://fee.org/articles/the-economic-way-of-thinking-part-6/

[iv] Manson, Mark. No, You Can't Have It All. Mark Manson. 2014. https://markmanson.net/you-cant-have-it-all

[v] Prince, J. Dyneley (July 1904). "Review: The Code of Hammurabi". The American Journal of Theology. The University of Chicago Press. 8 (3): 601–609. doi:10.1086/478479. JSTOR 3153895

[vi] Manson, Mark. No, You Can't Have It All. Mark Manson. 2014. https://markmanson.net/you-cant-have-it-all

[vii] Boyd, John. Zimbardo, Philip. *The Time Paradox: Using the New Psychology of Time to Your Advantage*. Atria Books. 2008.

[viii] Mehrabian, Albert. Albert Mehrabian Communication Studies. IOJT. 2013. http://www.iojt-

dc2013.org/~/media/Microsites/Files/IOJT/11042
013-Albert-Mehrabian-Communication-
Studies.ashx

[ix] Dean, Jeremy, PhD. Busting The Myth 93% of
Communication is Nonverbal. PsyBlog. 2007.
https://www.spring.org.uk/2007/05/busting-
myth-93-of-communication-is.php

[x] Pease, Allan. Pease, Barbara. *The Definitive Book
of Body Language: The Hidden Meaning Behind
People's Gestures and Expressions*. Bantam. 2006.

[xi] Pease, Allan. Pease, Barbara. *The Definitive
Book of Body Language: The Hidden Meaning
Behind People's Gestures and Expressions*.
Bantam. 2006.

[xii] Pease, Allan. Pease, Barbara. *The Definitive
Book of Body Language: The Hidden Meaning
Behind People's Gestures and Expressions*.
Bantam. 2006.

[xiii] Harvard Health Publishing. Understanding the
stress response. Harvard Health Publishing. 2018.
https://www.health.harvard.edu/staying-
healthy/understanding-the-stress-response

[xiv] Robinson, Lawrence. Smith, Melinda. Segal,
Robert. Stress Management. Helpfulguide. 2018.
https://www.helpguide.org/articles/stress/stress-
management.htm

[xv] Thoits, Peggy A. "Stress, Coping, and Social
Support Processes: Where Are We? What Next?"
Journal of Health and Social Behavior, 1995, 53-
79. http://www.jstor.org/stable/2626957

[xvi] Squier, Chemmie. Why Do We Get So Obsessed With 'Likes' On Social Media? Grazia Daily. 2016. https://graziadaily.co.uk/life/opinion/care-likes-social-media/

[xvii] Liden, Matt. 8 Buddhist Tips For Dealing With Anger. Study Buddhism. 2018. https://studybuddhism.com/en/essentials/how-to/8-buddhist-tips-for-dealing-with-anger

[xviii] Rosenberg, Marshall B. PhD. Nonviolent Communication. PuddleDancer Press; Third Edition. 2015.

[xix] Maslow, A. H. (1943). A theory of human motivation. Psychological Review, 50(4), 370-396. http://dx.doi.org/10.1037/h0054346

[xx] Crowther, Bosley. Walt Disney. Encyclopedia Britannica. 2018. https://www.britannica.com/biography/Walt-Disney

[xxi] Sterner, Thomas M. The Practicing Mind. New World Library. 2012.

[xxii] Sterner, Thomas M. The Practicing Mind. New World Library. 2012.

[xxiii] Schwarzenegger, Arnold. Total Recall. Simon&Schuster. 2013.